The Dangers Of Practical Magic

And How Names Are Symbols

H. P. Blavatsky

SECTION VI.

The Dangers of Practical Magic.

———

MAGIC is a dual power: nothing is easier than to turn it into Sorcery; *an evil thought suffices for it*. Therefore while theoretical Occultism is harmless, and may do good, practical Magic, or the fruits of the Tree of Life and Knowledge,* or otherwise the "Science of Good and Evil," is fraught with dangers and perils. For the study of theoretical Occultism there are, no doubt, a number of works that may be read with profit, besides such books as the *Finer Forces of Nature*, etc., the *Zohar*, *Sepher Jetzirah*, *The Book of Enoch*, Franck's *Kabalah*, and many Hermetic treatises. These are scarce in European languages, but works in Latin by the mediæval Philosophers, generally known as Alchemists and Rosicrucians, are plentiful. But even the perusal of these may prove dangerous for the unguided student. If approached without the right key to them, and if the student is unfit, owing to mental incapacity, for Magic, and is thus unable to discern the Right from the Left Path, let him take our advice and leave this study alone; he will only bring on himself and on his family un-expected woes and sorrows, never suspecting whence they come, nor what are the powers awakened by his mind being bent on them. Works for advanced students are many, but these can be placed at the disposal of only sworn or "pledged" chelâs (disciples), those who have pronounced the ever-binding oath, and who are, therefore, helped and protected. For all other purposes, well-intentioned as such works may

---

* Some Symbologists, relying on the correspondence of numbers and the symbols of certain things and personages, refer these "secrets" to the mystery of generation. But it is more than this. The glyph of the "Tree of Knowledge of Good and Evil" has no doubt a phallic and sexual element in it, as has the "Woman and the Serpent"; but it has also a psychical and spiritual significance. Symbols are meant to yield more than one meaning.

be, they can only mislead the unwary and guide them imperceptibly to Black Magic or Sorcery—if to nothing worse.

The mystic characters, alphabets and numerals found in the divisions and sub-divisions of the *Great Kabalah*, are, perhaps, the most dangerous portions in it, and especially the numerals. We say dangerous, because they are the most prompt to produce effects and results, and this with or without the experimenter's will, even without his knowledge. Some students are apt to doubt this statement, simply because after manipulating these numerals they have failed to notice any dire physical manifestation or result. Such results would be found the least dangerous: it is the moral causes produced and the various events developed and brought to an unforeseen crisis, that would testify to the truth of what is now stated had the lay students only the power of discernment.

The point of departure of that special branch of the Occult teaching known as the "Science of Correspondences," numerical or literal or alphabetical, has for its epigraph with the Jewish and Christian Kabalists, the two mis-interpreted verses which say that God

ordered all things in number, measure and weight;[*]

and:

He created her in the Holy Ghost, and saw her, and numbered her, and measured her.[†]

But the Eastern Occultists have another epigraph: "*Absolute Unity, x, within number and plurality.*" Both the Western and the Eastern students of the Hidden Wisdom hold to this axiomatic truth. Only the latter are perhaps more sincere in their confessions. Instead of putting a mask on their Science, they show her face openly, even if they do veil carefully her heart and soul before the inappreciative public and the profane, who are ever ready to abuse the most sacred truths for their own selfish ends. But Unity is the real basis of the Occult Sciences—physical and metaphysical. This is shown even by Éliphas Lévi, the learned Western Kabalist, inclined as he is to be rather jesuitical. He says:

Absolute Unity is the supreme and final reason of things. Therefore, that reason can be neither one person, nor three persons; it is Reason, and pre-eminently Reason (*raison par excellence*).[‡]

---

* *Wisdom*, xi. 21. Douay version.
† *Ecclesiasticus*, i. 9. Douay version.
‡ *Dogme et Rituel de la Haute Magie*, i. 361.

The meaning of this Unity in Plurality in "God" or Nature, can be solved only by the means of transcendental methods, by numerals, as by the correspondences between soul and the Soul. Names, in the *Kabalah*, as in the *Bible*, such as Jehovah, Adam Kadmon, Eve, Cain, Abel, Enoch, are all of them more intimately connected, by geometrical and astronomical relations, with Physiology (or Phallicism) than with Theology or Religion. Little as people are as yet prepared to admit it, this will be shown to be a fact. If all those names are symbols for things hidden, as well as for those manifested, in the *Bible* as in the *Vedas*, their respective mysteries differ greatly. Plato's motto "God geometrises" was accepted by both Âryans and Jews; but while the former applied their Science of Correspondences to veil the most spiritual and sublime truths of Nature, the latter used their acumen to conceal only one—to them the most divine—of the mysteries of Evolution, namely, that of birth and generation, and then they deified the organs of the latter.

Apart from this, every cosmogony, from the earliest to the latest, is based upon, interlinked with, and most closely related to, numerals and geometric figures. Questioned by an Initiate, these figures and numbers will yield numerical values based on the integral values of the Circle— "the secret habitat of the ever-invisible Deity" as the Alchemists have it—as they will yield every other Occult particular connected with such mysteries, whether anthropographical, anthropological, cosmic, or psychical. "In reuniting Ideas to Numbers, we can operate upon Ideas in the same way as upon Numbers, and arrive at the Mathematics of Truth," writes an Occultist, who shows his great wisdom in desiring to remain unknown.

Any Kabalist well acquainted with the Pythagorean system of numerals and geometry can demonstrate that the metaphysical views of Plato were based upon the strictest mathematical principles. "True mathematics," says the *Magicon*, "is something with which all higher sciences are connected; common mathematics is but a deceitful phantasmagoria, whose much praised infallibility only arises from this—that materials, conditions and references are made to foundation." . . .

The cosmological theory of numerals which Pythagoras learned in India, and from the Egyptian Hierophants, is alone able to reconcile the two units, matter and spirit, and cause each to demonstrate the other mathematically. The sacred numbers of the universe in their esoteric combination can alone solve the great problem, and explain the theory of radiation and the cycle of the emanations. The lower orders, before they develop into higher ones, must emanate from the higher spiritual ones, and when arrived at the turning-point, be reäbsorbed into the infinite.*

It is upon these true Mathematics that the knowledge of the Kosmos and of all mysteries rests, and to one acquainted with them, it is the easiest thing possible to prove that both Vaidic and Biblical structures are based upon "God-in-Nature" and "Nature-in-God," as the radical law. Therefore, this law—as everything else immutable and fixed in eternity—could find a correct expression only in those purest transcendental Mathematics referred to by Plato, especially in Geometry as transcendentally applied. *Revealed* to men—we fear not and will not retract the expression—in this geometrical and symbolical garb, Truth has grown and developed into additional symbology, invented by man for the wants and better comprehension of the masses of mankind that came too late in their cyclic devolopment and evolution to have shared in the primitive knowledge, and would never have grasped it otherwise. If later on, the clergy—crafty and ambitious of power in every age—anthropomorphised and degraded abstract ideals, as well as the real and divine Beings who do exist in Nature, and are the Guardians and Protectors of our manvantaric world and period, the fault and guilt rests with those would-be leaders, not with the masses.

But the day has come when the gross conceptions of our forefathers during the Middle Ages can no longer satisfy the thoughtful religionist. The mediæval Alchemist and Mystic are now transformed into the sceptical Chemist and Physicist; and most of them are found to have turned away from truth, on account of the purely anthropomorphic ideas, the gross Materialism, of the forms in which it is presented to them. Therefore, future generations have either to be gradually initiated into the truths underlying Exoteric Religions, including their own, or be left to break the feet of clay of the last of the gilded idols. No educated man or woman would turn away from any of the now called "superstitions," which they believe to be based on nursery tales and ignorance, if they could only see the basis of fact that underlies every "superstition." But let them once learn for a certainty that there is hardly a claim in the Occult Sciences that is not founded on philosophical and scientific facts in Nature, and they will pursue the study of those Sciences with the same, if not with greater, ardour than that they have expended in shunning them. This cannot be achieved at

---

* *Isis Unveiled*, i. 6, 7.

once, for to benefit mankind such truths have to be revealed gradually and with great caution, the public mind not being prepared for them. However much the Agnostics of our age may find themselves in the mental attitude demanded by Modern Science, people are always apt to cling to their old hobbies so long as the remembrance of them lasts. They are like the Emperor Julian—called the Apostate, because he loved truth too well to accept aught else—who, though in his last Theophany he beheld his beloved Gods as pale, worn-out, and hardly discernible shadows, nevertheless clung to them. Let, then, the world cling to its Gods, to whatever plane or realm they may belong. The true Occultist would be guilty of high treason to mankind, were he to break forever the old deities before he could replace them with the whole and un-adulterated truth—and this he cannot do as yet. Nevertheless, the reader may be allowed to learn at least the alphabet of that truth. He may be shown, at any rate, what the Gods and Goddesses of the Pagans, denounced as demons by the Church, are not, if he cannot learn the whole and final truth as to what they are. Let him assure himself that the Hermetic "Tres Matres," and the "Three Mothers" of the *Sepher Jetzirah* are one and the same thing; that they are no Demon-Goddesses, but Light, Heat, and Electricity, and then, perchance, the learned classes will spurn them no longer. After this, the Rosicrucian Illuminati may find followers even in the Royal Academies, which will be more prepared, perhaps, than they are now, to admit the grand truths of archaic Natural Philosophy, especially when their learned members shall have assured themselves that, in the dialect of Hermes, the "Three Mothers" stand as symbols for the whole of the forces or agencies which have a place assigned to them in the modern system of the "correlation of forces."* Even the polytheism of the "superstitious" Brâhman and idolater shows its *raison d' être*, since the three Shaktis of the three great Gods, Brahmâ, Vishnu, and Shiva, are identical with the "Three Mothers" of the monotheistic Jew.

The whole of the ancient religious and mystical literature is symboli-cal. The *Books of Hermes*, the *Zohar*, the *Ya-Yakav*, the Egyptian *Book*

---

* "Synesius mentions books of stone which he found in the temple of Memphis, on one of which was engraved the following sentence: 'One *nature* delights in another, one nature overcomes another, one nature overrules another, and the whole of them are *one*.'"

"The inherent restlessness of matter is embodied in the saying of Hermes: 'Action is the life of Phta'; and Orpheus calls nature πολυμήχανος μάτηρ, 'the mother that makes many things,' or the ingenious, the contriving, the inventive mother."—*Isis Unveiled*, i. 257.

of the Dead, the *Vedas*, the *Upanishads*, and the *Bible*, are as full of symbolism as are the Nabathean revelations of the Chaldaic Qù-tàmy; it is a loss of time to ask which is the earliest; all are simply different versions of the one primeval Record of prehistoric knowledge and revelation.

The first four chapters of *Genesis* contain the synopsis of all the rest of the *Pentateuch*, being only the various versions of the same thing in different allegorical and symbolical applications. Having discovered that the Pyramid of Cheops with all its measurements is to be found contained in its minutest details in the structure of Solomon's Temple; and having ascertained that the biblical names Shem, Ham and Japhet are determinative

of pyramid measures, in connection with the 600-year period of Noah and the 500-year period of Shem, Ham and Japhet: . . . the term "Sons of Elohim" and "Daughters" of H-Adam, [are] for one thing astronomical terms,*

the author of the very curious work already mentioned—a book very little known in Europe, we regret to say—seems to see nothing in his discovery beyond the presence of Mathematics and Metrology in the *Bible*. He also arrives at most unexpected and extraordinary conclusions, such as are very little warranted by the facts discovered. His impression seems to be that because the Jewish biblical names are all astronomical, therefore the Scriptures of all the other nations can be "only this and nothing more." But this is a great mistake of the erudite and wonderfully acute author of *The Source of Measures*, if he really thinks so. The "Key to the Hebrew-Egyptian Mystery" un-locks but a certain portion of the hieratic writings of these two nations, and leaves those of other peoples untouched. His idea is that the *Kabalah* "is only that sublime Science upon which Masonry is based"; in fact he regards Masonry as the substance of the *Kabalah*, and the latter as the "rational basis of the Hebrew text of Holy Writ." About this we will not argue with the author. But why should all those who may have found in the *Kabalah* something beyond "the sublime Science" upon which Masonry is alleged to have been built, be held up to public contempt?

In its exclusiveness and one-sidedness such a conclusion is pregnant with future misconceptions and is absolutely wrong. In its unchari-table criticism it throws a slur upon the "Divine Science" itself.

---

* *Source of Measures*, p. x.

The *Kabalah* is indeed "of the essence of Masonry," but it is dependent on Metrology only in one of its aspects, the less Esoteric, as even Plato made no secret that the Deity was ever geometrising. For the uninitiated, however learned and endowed with genius they may be, the *Kabalah*, which treats only of "the garment of God," or the *veil* and *cloak* of truth,

is built from the ground upward with a practical application to present uses.*

Or in other words represents an exact Science only on the terrestrial plane. To the initiated, the Kabalistic Lord descends from the primeval Race generated spiritually from the "Mind-born Seven." Having reached the Earth the Divine Mathematics—a synonym for Magic in his day, as we are told by Josephus—veiled her face. Hence the most important secret yet yielded by her in our modern day is the identity of the old Roman measures and the present British measures, of the Hebrew-Egyptian cubit and the Masonic inch.†

The discovery is most wonderful, and has led to further and minor unveilings of various riddles in reference to Symbology and biblical names. It is thoroughly understood and proven, as shown by Nachanides, that in the days of Moses the initial sentence in *Genesis* was made to read *B'rash ithbara Elohim*, or "In the head-source [or Mûlaprakriti—the Rootless Root] developed [or evolved] the Gods [Elohim], the heavens and the earth;" whereas it is now, owing to the Massora and theological cunning, transformed into *B'rashith bara Elohim*, or, "In the beginning God created the heavens and the earth"—which word juggling alone has led to materialistic anthropomorphism and dualism.‖ How many more similar instances may not be found in the *Bible*, the last and latest of the Occult works of antiquity? There is no longer any doubt in the mind of the Occultist, that, notwithstanding its form and outward meaning, the *Bible*—as explained by the *Zohar* or *Midrash*, the *Yetzirah* (Book of Creation) and the *Commentary on the Ten Sephiroth* (by Azariel Ben Manachem of the XIIth century)—is part and parcel of the Secret Doctrine of the Âryans, which explains in the same manner the *Vedas* and all other allegorical books. The *Zohar*, in teaching that the Impersonal One Cause manifests in the Universe through Its Emanations, the Sephiroth—that Universe being in its

---

* *Masonic Review*, July 1886.
† See *Source of Measures*, pp. 47—50, *et pass.*

totality simply the veil woven from the Deity's own substance—is undeniably the copy and faithful echo of the earliest *Vedas*. Taken by itself, without the additional help of the Vaidic and of Brâhmanical literature in general, the *Bible* will never yield the universal secrets of Occult Nature. The cubits, inches, and measures of this physical plane will never solve the problems of the world on the spiritual plane —for Spirit can neither be weighed nor measured. The working out of these problems is reserved for the "mystics and the dreamers" who alone are capable of accomplishing it.

Moses was an initiated priest, versed in all the mysteries and the Occult knowledge of the Egyptian temples—hence thoroughly acquainted with primitive Wisdom. It is in the latter that the symbolical and astronomical meaning of that "Mystery of Mysteries," the Great Pyramid, has to be sought. And having been so familiar with the geometrical secrets that lay concealed for long æons in her strong bosom—the measurements and proportions of the Kosmos, our little Earth included—what wonder that he should have made use of his knowledge? The Esoterism of Egypt was that of the whole world at one time. During the long ages of the Third Race it had been the heirloom, in common, of the whole of mankind, received from their Instructors, the "Sons of Light," the primeval Seven. There was a time also when the Wisdom-Religion was not symbolical, for it became Esoteric only gradually, the change being necessitated by misuse and by the Sorcery of the Atlanteans. For it was the "misuse" only, and not the use, of the divine gift that led the men of the Fourth Race to Black Magic and Sorcery, and finally to become "forgetful of Wisdom"; while those of the Fifth Race, the inheritors of the Rishis of the Tretâ Yuga, used their powers to atrophise such gifts in mankind in general, and then, as the "Elect Root," dispersed. Those who escaped the "Great Flood" preserved only its memory, and a belief founded on the knowledge of their direct fathers of one remove, that such a Science existed, and was now jealously guarded by the "Elect Root" exalted by Enoch. But there must again come a time when man shall once more become what he was during the second Yuga (age), when his probationary cycle shall be over and he shall gradually become what he was—semi-corporeal and pure. Does not Plato, the Initiate, tell us in the *Phædrus* all that man once was, and that which he may yet again become:

Before man's spirit sank into sensuality and became embodied through the loss of his wings, he lived among the Gods in the airy spiritual world where everything is true and pure.*

Elsewhere he speaks of the time when men did not perpetuate themselves, but lived as pure spirits.

Let those men of Science who feel inclined to laugh at this, themselves unravel the mystery of the origin of the first man.

Unwilling that his chosen people—chosen by him—should remain as grossly idolatrous as the profane masses that surrounded them, Moses utilised his knowledge of the cosmogonical mysteries of the Pyramid, to build upon it the Genesiacal Cosmogony in symbols and glyphs. This was more accessible to the minds of the *hoi polloi* than the abstruse truths taught to the educated in the sanctuaries. He invented nothing but the outward garb, added not one iota; but in this he merely followed the example of older nations and Initiates. If he clothed the grand truths revealed to him by his Hierophant under the most ingenious imagery, he did it to meet the requirements of the Israelites; that stiff-necked race would accept of no God unless He were as anthropomorphic as those of the Olympus; and he himself failed to foresee the times when highly educated statesmen would be defending the husks of the fruit of wisdom that grew and developed in him on Mount Sinai, when communing with his own personal God—his divine Self. Moses understood the great danger of delivering such truths to the selfish, for he understood the fable of Prometheus and remembered the past. Hence, he veiled them from the profanation of public gaze and gave them out allegorically. And this is why his biographer says of him, that when he descended from Sinai,

Moses wist not that the skin of his face shone . . . and he put a veil upon his face.†

And so he "put a veil" upon the face of his *Pentateuch;* and to such an extent that, using orthodox chronology, only 3376 years after the event people begin to acquire a conviction that it is "a veil indeed." It is not the face of God or even of a Jehovah shining through; not even the face of Moses, but verily the faces of the later Rabbis.

No wonder if Clemens wrote in the *Stromateis* that:

Similar, then, to the Hebrew enigmas in respect to concealment are those of the Egyptians also.‡

---

* See Cary's translation, pp. 3**. 3**.
† *Exodus,* xxxiv. 29, 33.
‡ *Op. cit.,* V. vii.

CPSIA information can be obtained
at www.ICGtesting.com
Printed in the USA
LVRC021950221120
672361LV00027BB/697

9 781163 005798